Leveled Texts

For Kindergarten

Consultants

Kristy Stark, M.A.Ed.
Reading Level Consultant
Long Beach, California

Wendy Conklin, M.A.
Gifted Education Consultant
Round Rock, Texas

Dennis Benjamin
Special Education Consultant
Prince William County Public Schools, Virginia

Marcela von Vacano
English Language Learner Consultant
Arlington County Schools, Virginia

Publishing Credits

Corinne Burton, M.A.Ed., *President*; Conni Medina, M.A.Ed., *Managing Editor*;
Emily Rossman Smith, M.A.Ed., *Content Director*; Angela Johnson, M.F.A., M.S.Ed., *Editor*;
Robin Erickson, *Multimedia Designer*; Kevin Pham, *Production Artist*;
Danielle Deovlet, *Assistant Editor*

Image Credits

pp.35, 37, 39 Holly Homer; pp.101, 103, 105 kali9/Getty Images; pp.125, 127, 129 (upper left) LOC [LC-DIG-pga-03757], (upper and bottom right) North Wind Pictures Archives. (lower left) LOC [LC-USZC4-2737]; All other images from iStock, Shutterstock, or the public domain.

Standards

© 2004 Mid-continent Research for Education and Learning (McREL)
© 2006 Teachers of English to Speakers of Other Languages, Inc. (TESOL)
© Copyright 2010. National Governors Association Center for Best Practices and Council of Chief State School Officers. All rights reserved.

Shell Education

A division of Teacher Created Materials
5301 Oceanus Drive
Huntington Beach, CA 92649–1030
http://www.tcmpub.com/shell-education
ISBN 978–1–4258–1627–8
©2016 Shell Educational Publishing, Inc.
Printed in USA. WOR004

Table of Contents

What Is Differentiation?

Over the past few years, classrooms have evolved into diverse pools of learners. Gifted students, English language learners, special-needs students, high achievers, underachievers, and average students all come together to learn from one teacher. The teacher is expected to meet their diverse needs in one classroom. It brings back memories of the one-room schoolhouse during early American history. Not too long ago, lessons were designed to be one size fits all. It was thought that students in the same grade learned in similar ways. Today, teachers know that viewpoint to be faulty. Students have different learning styles, come from different cultures, experience a variety of emotions, and have varied interests. For each subject, they also differ in academic readiness. At times, the challenges teachers face can be overwhelming, as they struggle to figure out how to create learning environments that address the differences they find in their students.

What is differentiation? Carol Ann Tomlinson (2014, 1) describes the challenge of differentiation as reaching out to "students who span the spectrum of learning readiness, personal interests, and culturally shaped ways of seeing and speaking about and experiencing the world." Differentiation can be carried out by any teacher who keeps the learners at the forefront of his or her instruction. The effective teacher asks, "What am I going to do to shape instruction to meet the needs of all my learners?" One method or methodology will not reach all students.

Differentiation encompasses what is taught, how it is taught, and the products students create to show what they have learned. When differentiating curriculum, teachers become the organizers of learning opportunities within the classroom environment. These categories are often referred to as content, process, and product.

- **Content:** Differentiating the content means to put more depth into the curriculum through organizing the curriculum concepts and structure of knowledge.

- **Process:** Differentiating the process requires the use of varied instructional techniques and materials to enhance the learning of students.

- **Product:** When products are differentiated, cognitive development and the students' abilities to express themselves improve.

Teachers should differentiate content, process, and products according to students' characteristics. These characteristics include students' readiness, learning styles, and interests.

- **Readiness:** If a learning experience aligns closely with students' previous skills and understanding of a topic, they will learn better.

- **Learning styles:** Teachers should create assignments that allow students to complete work according to their personal preferences and styles.

- **Interests:** If a topic sparks excitement in the learners, then students will become involved in learning and better remember what is taught.

4

How to Differentiate Using This Product

The leveled texts in this series help teachers differentiate language arts, mathematics, science, and social studies content for students. Each section has five passages, and each passage is written at three different reading levels. (See page 8 for more information.) While these texts are written on three reading levels, all levels remain strong in presenting subject-specific content and vocabulary. Teachers can focus on the same content standard or objective for the whole class, but individual students can access the content at their instructional levels rather than at their frustration levels.

Determining your students' instructional reading levels is the first step in the process. It is important to assess their reading abilities often so students are instructed on the correct levels. Below are suggested ways to use this resource, as well as other resources in your building, to determine students' reading levels.

- **Running records:** While your class is doing independent work, pull your below-grade-level students aside, one at a time. Individually, have them read aloud the lowest level of a text from this product (the circle level) as you record any errors they make on your own copy of the text. Assess their accuracy and fluency by marking the words they say incorrectly and listening for fluent reading. Use your judgment to determine whether students seem frustrated as they read. Following the reading, ask comprehension questions to assess their understanding of the material. If students read accurately and fluently and comprehend the material, move them up to the next level and repeat the process. As a general guideline, students reading below 90% accuracy are likely to feel frustrated as they read. There are also a variety of published reading assessment tools that can be used to assess students' reading levels using the oral running record format.

- **Refer to other resources:** You can also use other reading level placement tests, such as the Developmental Reading Assessment or the Qualitative Reading Inventory, to determine your students' reading levels. Then, use the chart on page 8 to determine which text level is the best fit for each student.

Teachers can also use the texts in this series to scaffold the content for their students. At the beginning of the year, students at the lowest reading levels may need focused teacher guidance. As the year progresses, teachers can begin giving students multiple levels of the same text to allow them to work independently to improve their comprehension. This means that each student would have a copy of the text at his or her independent reading level and a copy of the text one level above that. As students read the instructional-level texts, they can use the lower texts to better understand the difficult vocabulary. By scaffolding the content in this way, teachers can support students as they move up through the reading levels. This will encourage students to work with texts that are closer to the grade level at which they will be tested.

General Information About Student Populations

Below-Grade-Level Students

As with all student populations, students who are below grade level span a spectrum of abilities. Some of these students have individualized education plans, while others do not. Some below-grade-level students are English language learners (ELLs), while others are native English speakers. Selected students receive intervention and/or support services, while many other students do not qualify for such services. The shift toward inclusive classrooms has caused an increase in the number of below-grade-level students in the general education classrooms.

These students, regardless of abilities, are often evaluated on the same learning objectives as their on-grade-level peers, and their learning becomes the responsibility of classroom teachers. The following questions come to mind: How do classroom teachers provide this population with "access to texts that allows them to perform like good, proficient readers" (Fountas and Pinnell 2012, 2)? How do classroom teachers differentiate for this population without limiting access to content, grade-level vocabulary, and language? Pages 132–136 give tangible strategies to support this student population.

On-Grade-Level Students

Often, on-grade-level students get overlooked when planning curriculum. More emphasis is placed on students who struggle and, at times, on those students who excel. Teachers spend time teaching basic skills and even go below grade level to ensure that all students are up to speed. While this is a noble thing and is necessary at times, in the midst of it all, the on-grade-level students can get lost in the shuffle. Providing activities that are too challenging can frustrate these students, and on the other hand, assignments that are too easy can seem tedious. The key to reaching this population successfully is to find the right level of activities and questions while keeping a keen eye on their diverse learning styles. Strategies can include designing activities based on the theory of multiple intelligences. Current brain research points to the success of active learning strategies. These strategies provoke strong positive emotions and use movement during the learning process to help these students learn more effectively. On-grade-level students also benefit from direct teaching of higher-level thinking skills. Keep the activities open ended so that these students can surprise you with all they know. The strategies described on pages 137–138 were specifically chosen because they are very effective for meeting the needs of on-grade-level students.

General Information About Student Populations *(cont.)*

Above-Grade-Level Students

All students should be learning, growing, and expanding their knowledge in school. This includes above-grade-level students, too. But they will not grow and learn unless someone challenges them with appropriate curriculum. In her book *Differentiating the Language Arts for High Ability Learners*, Joyce Van Tassel-Baska (2003, 2) stresses that "the level of curriculum for gifted learners must be adapted to their needs for advancement, depth, and complexity." Doing this can be overwhelming at times, even for experienced teachers. However, there are some strategies that teachers can use to challenge the gifted population. These strategies include open-ended questions, student-directed learning, and extension assignments. See pages 138–140 for more information about each of these strategies.

English Language Learners

Acquiring a second language is a lengthy process that integrates listening, speaking, reading, and writing. Students who are newcomers to the English language are not able to deeply process information until they have mastered a certain number of language structures and vocabulary words. Even after mastering these structures, English language learners need to be immersed in rich verbal and textual language daily in school. Students may learn social language in one or two years. However, academic language takes up to eight years for most students to learn. Teaching academic language requires good planning and effective implementation. Pacing, or the rate at which information is presented, is another important component in this process. English language learners need to hear the same words in context several times, and they need to practice structures to internalize the words. Reviewing and summarizing what was taught are absolutely necessary for English language learners' success in the future (August and Shanahan 2006). See pages 141–143 for more information about each of the strategies mentioned here.

How to Use This Product

Readability Chart

Title of the Text	Circle	Square	Triangle
Birds and Bugs	no text	labels	2.0
My Birthday Party	no text	labels	2.0
All About the Sun	no text	labels	2.2
Workers Who Take Care of Me	no text	labels	2.2
Simple Tools	no text	labels	2.2
The Bakery	no text	labels	2.3
In the Garden	no text	labels	2.2
Farm Animals	no text	labels	2.2
Recess Time	no text	labels	2.3
Fun in the Sun	no text	labels	2.0
On Land	no text	labels	2.0
What Do Living Things Need?	no text	labels	2.2
Baby Animals	no text	labels	2.0
Solid or Liquid?	no text	labels	2.2
Changing Weather	no text	labels	2.0
I Am a Good Friend	no text	labels	2.2
Using Money	no text	labels	2.2
Map It!	no text	labels	2.2
Rules at Home	no text	labels	2.1
George Washington	no text	labels	2.0

Correlation to Standards

The Every Student Succeeds Act (ESSA) mandates that all states adopt challenging academic standards that help students meet the goal of college and career readiness. While many states already adopted academic standards prior to ESSA, the act continues to hold states accountable for detailed and comprehensive standards.

Shell Education is committed to producing educational materials that are research and standards based. In this effort, all products are correlated to the academic standards of the 50 states, the District of Columbia, and the Department of Defense Dependent Schools. Shell Education uses the Mid-continent Research for Education and Learning (McREL) Compendium to create standards correlations. Each year, McREL analyzes state standards and revises the compendium. By following this procedure, they are able to produce a general compilation of national standards. A correlation report customized for your state can be printed directly from the following website: **www.tcmpub.com/administrators/correlations/**.

How to Use This Product *(cont.)*

Components of the Product

The Leveled Texts

- There are 20 topics in this book. Each topic is leveled to three different reading levels. The images and fonts used for each level within a topic are the same.

- Behind each page number, you'll see a shape. These shapes indicate the reading levels of each piece so that you can make sure students are working with the correct texts. The circle level pieces have images only with no text so they can be used by nonreaders. The square level pieces are for very early readers and use labels only. See the chart on page 8 for the specific level of each triangle text.

no text   labels   Levels 2.0–2.3

Comprehension Activities

- Each level of the texts includes a comprehension activity. Like the texts, the comprehension activities were created with nonreaders and early readers in mind. They are written to allow all students to be successful within a whole-class discussion of the content. The activities are closely linked among the three levels so that students will be able to participate in the conversations about the texts. The below-grade-level students might focus on the images, while the above-grade-level students can delve deeper into the meanings of the sentences and images.

How to Use This Product *(cont.)*

Tips for Managing the Product

How to Prepare the Texts

- When you copy these texts, be sure you set your copier to copy photographs. Run a few test pages and adjust the contrast as necessary. If you want the students to be able to appreciate the images, you will need to carefully prepare the texts for them.

- You also have full-color versions of the texts provided in PDF form on the Digital Resource CD. (See page 144 for more information.) Depending on how many copies you need to make, printing full-color versions and/or copying from a full-color version might work best for you.

- Keep in mind that you should copy two-sided to two-sided if you pull the pages out of the book. The shapes behind the page numbers will help you keep the pages organized as you prepare them.

Distributing the Texts

- Some teachers wonder about how to hand out the texts within one classroom. They worry that students will feel insulted if they do not get the same papers as their neighbors. The first step in dealing with these texts is to set up your classroom as a place where all students learn at their individual instructional levels. Making this clear as a fact of life in your classroom is key. Otherwise, the students may constantly ask about why their work is different. You do not need to get into the technicalities of the reading levels. Just state it as a fact that every student will not be working on the same assignment every day. If you do this, then passing out the varied levels is not a problem. Just pass them to the correct students as you circle the room.

- If you would rather not have students openly aware of the differences in the texts, you can try these strategies for passing out the materials.

  - Make a pile in your hands from the circle to triangle level. Put your fingers between the levels. As you approach each student, you pull from the correct section to meet his/her reading level. If you do not hesitate too much in front of each desk, the students will probably not notice.

  - Begin the class period with an opening activity. Put the texts in different places around the room. As students work quietly, circulate and direct students to the correct locations for retrieving the texts you want them to use.

  - Organize the texts in small piles by seating arrangement so that when you arrive at a group of desks you will have just the levels you need.

Birds and Bugs

Name: _____ Date: _____

Birds and Bugs *(cont.)*

Directions: Draw a bird or bug you
have seen.

Birds and Bugs

one bird

two bugs

three birds

four bugs

Name: _____ Date: _____

Birds and Bugs (cont.)

Directions: Draw a bird or bug you have seen. Label your picture.

- -

Birds and Bugs

One owl is sitting on a branch.

Two bugs are resting on a leaf.

Three parrots are perched together.

Four ladybugs are eating leaves.

Name: _____ Date: _____

Birds and Bugs (cont.)

Directions: Draw a bird or bug you have seen. Write about your picture.

[Drawing box]

_____

- -

_____

_____

- -

_____

My Birthday Party

Name: _____ Date: _____

My Birthday Party (cont.)

Directions: Draw friends at a birthday party.

My Birthday Party

my birthday

friends

gifts

cupcakes

Name: _____ Date: _____

My Birthday Party *(cont.)*

Directions: Draw what friends can do at a birthday party. Label your picture.

My Birthday Party

It is my birthday party.

My party has friends.

My party has gifts.

My party has cupcakes.

Name: _____ Date: _____

My Birthday Party *(cont.)*

Directions: Draw friends at a birthday party. Write about your picture.

- -

- -

All About the Sun

Name: _____ Date: _____

All About the Sun (cont.)

Directions: Draw one thing the sun can do.

All About the Sun

shines

melts

sprouts

grows

Name: _____ Date: _____

All About the Sun (cont.)

Directions: Draw one thing the sun can do. Label your picture.

_____

_ _

_____

All About the Sun

The sun is warm.
It shines on trees.

The sun melts ice
into water.

The sun sprouts
buds into plants,
such as flowers
and fruits.

The sun helps
leaves grow bigger
to collect even
more sunlight.

Name: _____ Date: _____

All About the Sun (cont.)

Directions: Draw one thing the sun can do. Write about your picture.

_____

- -

_____

_____

- -

_____

Workers Who Take Care of Me

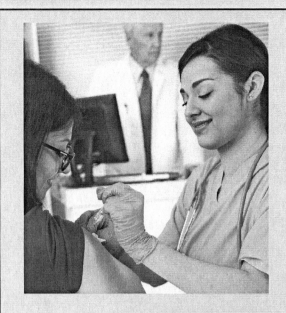

Name: _____ Date: _____

Workers Who Take Care of Me (cont.)

Directions: Draw one worker who takes care of you.

Workers Who Take Care of Me

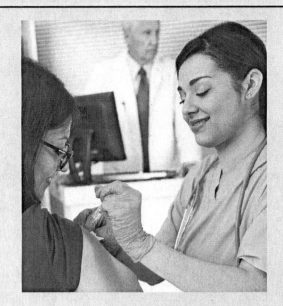

health worker

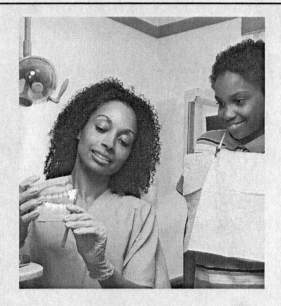

health worker

safety worker

safety worker

Name: _____ Date: _____

Workers Who Take Care of Me (cont.)

Directions: Draw one worker who takes care of you. Label the worker as *health worker* or *safety worker*.

_____

– –

_____

Workers Who Take Care of Me

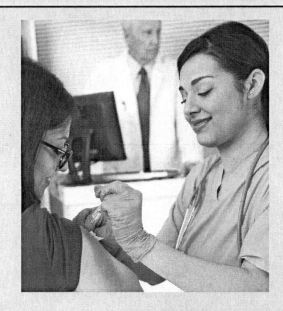

This is a worker who takes care of my health.

This is a worker who takes care of my teeth.

This is a safety worker and a dog.

This is a safety worker.

Name: _____ Date: _____

Workers Who Take Care of Me (cont.)

Directions: Draw one worker who takes care of you. Write about the worker.

_____

- -

_____

- -

_____

Simple Tools

Name: _____ Date: _____

Simple Tools (cont.)

Directions: Draw a tool you use.

Simple Tools

tool

tool at work

tool

tool at work

Name: _____ Date: _____

Simple Tools (cont.)

Directions: Draw a tool you use. Label your picture with the name of the tool.

_____

– –

_____

Simple Tools

This tool is a wheel. Wheels help pull heavy things easily.

This shows the tool at work in a wagon.

This tool is a pulley. It helps you lift heavy things easily.

This shows the tool at work pulling a bucket into a treehouse.

Name: _____ Date: _____

Simple Tools (cont.)

Directions: Draw a tool you use. Write about the tool.

_____

- -

_____

_____

- -

_____

The Bakery

Name: _____ Date: _____

The Bakery (cont.)

Directions: Draw something you eat from a bakery.

The Bakery

two desserts

one sold

four cakes

two sold

Name: _____ Date: _____

The Bakery (cont.)

Directions: Draw the treats that were sold. Label your picture.

The Bakery

There are two
desserts in
the store.

The store sells
one dessert to a
customer, so now it
has one dessert left.

There are four
cakes in the store.

The store sells
two cakes to a
customer, so now it
has two cakes left.

Name: _____ Date: _____

The Bakery (cont.)

Directions: Draw the treats left in the bakery. Label how many treats are left in the bakery.

In the Garden

Name: _____ Date: _____

In the Garden *(cont.)*

Directions: Draw something you might find in a garden.

In the Garden

two rabbits

three snails

four apples

eight ants

Name: _____ Date: _____

In the Garden (cont.)

Directions: Draw three snails and five apples. Circle the picture with the greater number.

In the Garden

There are two rabbits hiding in a meadow of tall grass.

There are three tiny snails perched on a leaf.

There are four apples that are ripe and ready to pick.

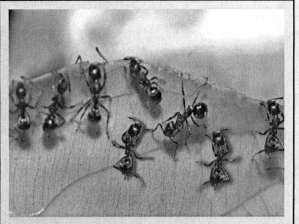

There are eight small ants nibbling on a lush green leaf.

Name: _____ Date: _____

In the Garden *(cont.)*

Directions: Draw three snails and five apples. Explain which number is greater.

_____

_____

_____

_____

Farm Animals

Name: _____ Date: _____

Farm Animals (cont.)

Directions: Draw an animal that is big.
Then draw an animal that is small.

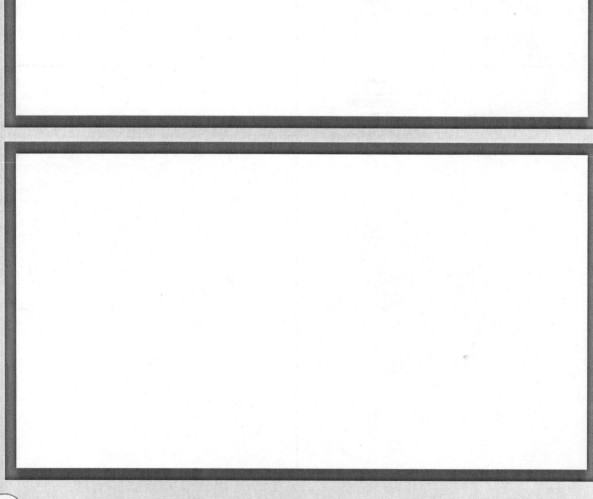

Farm Animals

big

small

small

big

Name: _____ Date: _____

Farm Animals *(cont.)*

Directions: Draw an animal that is big. Then draw an animal that is small. Label your pictures *big* and *small*.

Farm Animals

This cow walking in the meadow is big.

This fluffy yellow chick is small.

This rabbit in the meadow is small.

This horse prancing in the meadow is big.

Name: _____ Date: _____

Farm Animals (cont.)

Directions: Draw an animal that is big. Then draw an animal that is small. Write about the pictures.

Recess Time

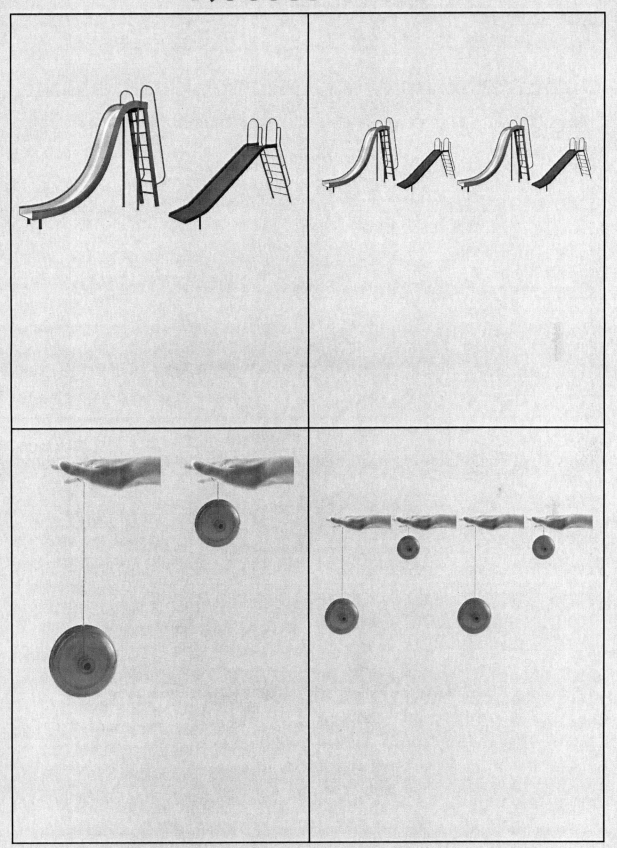

Name: _____ Date: _____

Recess Time *(cont.)*

Directions: Draw a slide. Then draw a circle.

Recess Time

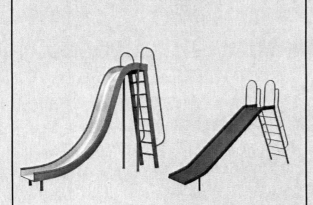

slides

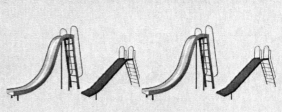

pattern

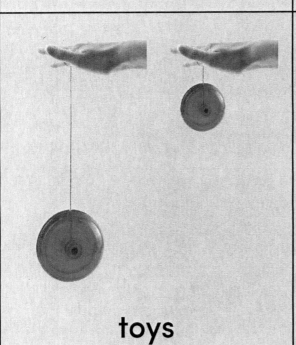

toys

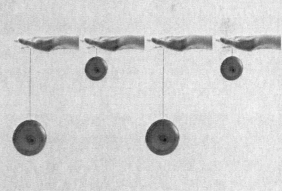

pattern

Name: _____ Date: _____

Recess Time (cont.)

Directions: Draw a pattern with shapes. Label the shapes in your pattern.

Recess Time

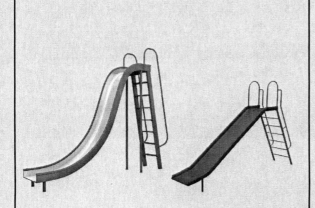

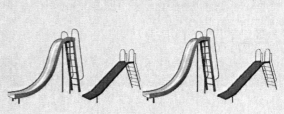

Slides at the park or school can be tall or short.

Tall and short slides can be used to make a pattern.

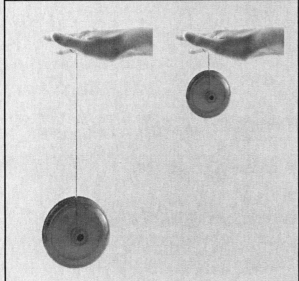

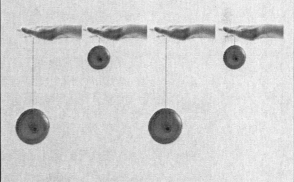

Toys come in different sizes that can be big or little.

Big and little toys can be used to make a pattern.

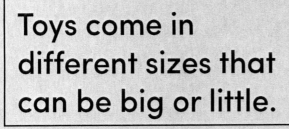

Name: _____ Date: _____

Recess Time (cont.)

Directions: Draw a pattern. Then explain your pattern.

_____

- -

_____

- -

_____

Fun in the Sun

Name: _____ Date: _____

Fun in the Sun (cont.)

Directions: Draw a picture to show how you have fun in the sun.

Fun in the Sun

one tube

two slides

two kids

three balls

Name: _____ Date: _____

Fun in the Sun (cont.)

Directions: Draw a picture to show how you have fun in the sun. Label your picture.

_____

– –

_____

Fun in the Sun

This girl is using one tube to help her float in the water.

There are two slides that twist and turn together.

There are two kids wearing goggles in the pool.

These kids are playing in the sand.

Name: _____ Date: _____

Fun in the Sun (cont.)

Directions: Draw a picture to show how you have fun in the sun with friends. Write a sentence about your picture.

_____

– –

_____

– –

_____

On Land

Name: _____ Date: _____

On Land (cont.)

Directions: Draw a picture of the land outside your home.

On Land

grassy

sandy

wet

dry

Name: _____ Date: _____

On Land (cont.)

Directions: Draw a picture of the land outside your home. Label your picture.

_____

- -

_____

On Land

The hilly, green land is grassy.

This desert land is very sandy.

This swampy land is wet.

This cracked, desert land is dry.

Name: _____ Date: _____

On Land (cont.)

Directions: Draw a picture of the land outside your home. Then write about your picture.

_____

- - - - - - - - - - - - - - - - - - -

_____

- - - - - - - - - - - - - - - - - - -

_____

What Do Living Things Need?

Name: _____ Date: _____

What Do Living Things Need? *(cont.)*

Directions: Draw a picture of something living things need.

What Do Living Things Need?

light

food

water

air

Name: _____ Date: _____

What Do Living Things Need? (cont.)

Directions: Draw a picture of something living things need. Label your picture.

What Do Living Things Need?

Living things need light from the sun.

Living things need to eat healthy food to survive.

Living things need to drink plenty of clean water.

Living things need to breathe fresh air.

Name: _____ Date: _____

What Do Living Things Need? (cont.)

Directions: Draw a picture of something living things need. Then explain your drawing.

_____

- -

_____

- -

_____

Baby Animals

Name: _____ Date: _____

Baby Animals (cont.)

Directions: Draw your favorite baby animal.

Baby Animals

two bears

one cub

two ducks

six ducklings

Name: _____ Date: _____

Baby Animals (cont.)

Directions: Draw your favorite baby animal. Label your picture.

_____

- -

_____

Baby Animals

There are two big adult bears.

They have one little, playful cub.

There are two friendly adult ducks.

They have six fluffy ducklings.

Name: _____ Date: _____

Baby Animals (cont.)

Directions: Draw your favorite baby animal. Explain why it is your favorite baby animal.

_____

- -

_____

_____

- -

_____

Solid or Liquid?

Name: _____ Date: _____

Solid or Liquid? *(cont.)*

Directions: Draw a picture of a solid or a liquid.

Solid or Liquid?

solid

liquid

solid

liquid

Name: _____ Date: _____

Solid or Liquid? *(cont.)*

Directions: Draw a picture of something. Label your picture *solid* or *liquid*.

_____

— — — — — — — — — — — — — — — — — — —

_____

Solid or Liquid?

This orange is in a solid state.

This orange juice is a liquid.

This frozen ice cream is in a solid state.

This melted ice cream is a liquid.

93

Name: _____ **Date:** _____

Solid or Liquid? *(cont.)*

Directions: Draw a picture of something. Then explain why it is a solid or a liquid.

_____

- -

_____

_____

- -

_____

Changing Weather

Name: _____ Date: _____

Changing Weather (cont.)

Directions: Draw a picture of your favorite type of weather.

Changing Weather

sun

clouds

rain

rainbow

Name: _____ Date: _____

Changing Weather (cont.)

Directions: Draw a picture of your favorite type of weather. Label your picture.

- -

Changing Weather

This is the warm, shining sun.

These are gray, dark clouds.

This is cold, wet rain falling heavily.

This is a bright, colorful rainbow.

Name: _____ Date: _____

Changing Weather (cont.)

Directions: Draw a picture of your favorite type of weather. Explain why it is your favorite type of weather.

- -

- -

I Am a Good Friend

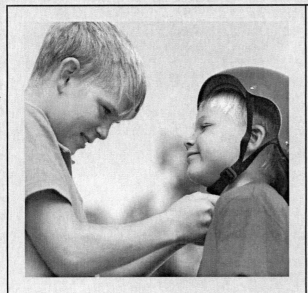

Name: _____ Date: _____

I Am a Good Friend (cont.)

Directions: Draw a picture of one of your good friends.

I Am a Good Friend

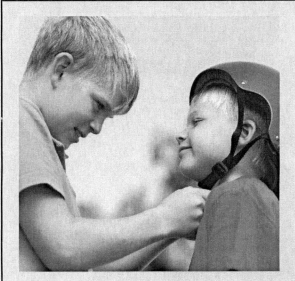

help

share

play

care

Name: _____ Date: _____

I Am a Good Friend (cont.)

Directions: Draw a picture of one of your good friends. Label the picture with your friend's name.

_____

- -

_____

I Am a Good Friend

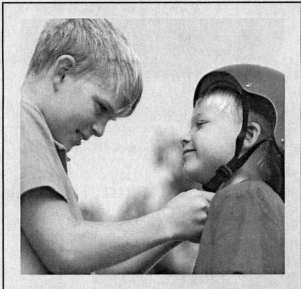

We help each other with different things.

We share our toys, so we can play.

We play together at recess and in the park.

We care about each other.

Name: _____ Date: _____

I Am a Good Friend (cont.)

Directions: Draw a picture of one of your good friends. Explain why he or she is a good friend.

_____

- -

_____

- -

_____

Using Money

Name: _____ Date: _____

Using Money (cont.)

Directions: Draw a picture to show how you use money.

Using Money

earn

count

save

spend

Name: _____ Date: _____

Using Money (cont.)

Directions: Draw a picture to show how you use money. Label your picture.

_____

- -

_____

Using Money

I earn money by selling lemonade.

I count my money.

I save some money.

I spend some money at the store.

Name: _____ Date: _____

Using Money (cont.)

Directions: Draw a picture to show how you use money. Then explain your picture.

_____

_____

_____

_____

_____

Map It!

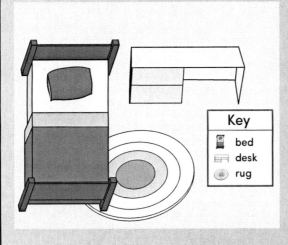

Key

🛏 bed
🗄 desk
◎ rug

Name: _____ Date: _____

Map It! (cont.)

Directions: Draw a map of your classroom.

Map It!

map

place

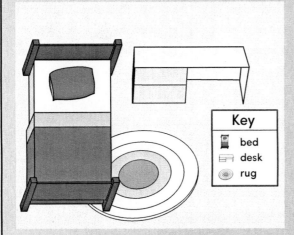

map

place

Name: _____ Date: _____

Map It! (cont.)

Directions: Draw a map of your classroom. Label things on your map.

Map It!

This is what a map looks like.

A map shows details about where to find a place.

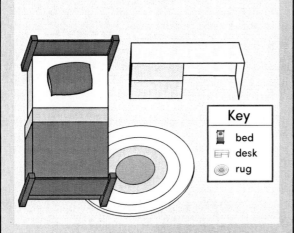

Key
- bed
- desk
- rug

This is another type of map.

The map shows what is inside this bedroom.

Name: _____ Date: _____

Map It! *(cont.)*

Directions: Draw a map of your classroom. Write about why we use maps.

_____

- -

_____

- -

_____

Rules at Home

Name: _____ Date: _____

Rules at Home (cont.)

Directions: Draw a picture of your family at home.

Rules at Home

fair

share

nice

help

Name: _____ Date: _____

Rules at Home (cont.)

Directions: Draw a picture of your family following the rules at home. Label your drawing.

_____

_ _ _ _ _ _ _ _ _ _ _ _ _ _ _

_____

Rules at Home

We have to be fair at home. When we play video games, we must make sure everyone gets a turn.

We have to share at home. When we use computers, we must share with our family members.

We have to be nice at home. We must show our family we care and spend time together.

We have to help at home. We can do chores such as laundry or cleaning.

Name: _____ Date: _____

Rules at Home (cont.)

Directions: Draw a picture of your family following the rules at home. Explain what they are doing.

_____

- -

_____

_____

- -

_____

George Washington

Name: _____ Date: _____

George Washington (cont.)

Directions: Draw a picture of a president.

George Washington

George
Washington

farmer

army

president

Name: _____ Date: _____

George Washington *(cont.)*

Directions: Draw a picture of a president. Label your drawing.

- -

George Washington

Meet George Washington.

He worked on a farm.

He led the army.

He was the first president.

Name: _____ Date: _____

George Washington (cont.)

Directions: Draw a picture of a president. Explain what the president does.

_____

- -

_____

- -

_____

References Cited

August, Diane and Timothy Shanahan. 2006. *Developing Literacy in Second-Language Learners: Report of the National Literacy Panel on Language-Minority Children and Youth.* Mahwah, New Jersey: Lawrence Erlbaum Associates, Inc.

Fountas, Irene and Gay Su Pinnell. 2012. *The Critical Role of Text Complexity in Teaching Children to Read.* Portsmouth, Virginia: Heinemann.

Naughton, Victoria M. 1993. "Creative Mapping for Content Reading." *Journal of Reading.* 37(4): 326–26.

Pearson, P. David, and Dale D. Johnson. 1978. *Teaching Reading Comprehension.* New York: Hold, Rinehart and Winston.

Tomlinson, Carol Ann. 2014. *The Differentiated Classroom. Responding to the Needs of All Learners, 2nd Edition.* Reston, Virginia: Association for Supervision and Curriculum Development.

Van Tassel-Baska, Joyce. 2003. "Differentiating the Language Arts for High Ability Learners, K–8. ERIC Digest." Arlington, Virginia: ERIC Clearinghouse on Disabilities and Gifted Education.

Vygotsky, Lev Semenovich. 1978. "Interaction Between Learning and Development." In *Mind in Society*, 79–91. Cambridge, Massachusetts: Harvard University Press.

Strategies for Using the Leveled Texts

Throughout this section are differentiation strategies that can be used with each leveled text to support reading comprehension for the students in your classroom.

Below-Grade-Level Students

Peek-a-boo Picture Walk

As a prereading strategy, have students take a picture walk. Picture walks allow students to infer and make predictions about the text before viewing or reading the passage. This strategy allows below-grade-level students to activate prior knowledge before viewing or reading texts. Students should look at one picture at a time, covering the other three images. This technique allows students to focus on one image so they can pay close attention to details while examining each picture. During the picture walk, infuse as many text-specific words as possible into the classroom discussion. (A sample list can be found on page 134.) Additionally, use the sample questions below to focus the picture walk.

- What is happening in this picture?
- What do you think will happen next?
- What do you think this text is about?
- What other pictures might fit in this set?

Predict and Learn

In conjunction with the picture walk, students can write or sketch their predictions on the Predict and Learn chart below. This strategy requires below-grade-level students to actively analyze texts before viewing or reading them and provides a reference for classroom discussions afterwards.

What I predict	What I learned

Strategies for Using the Leveled Texts *(cont.)*

Below-Grade-Level Students *(cont.)*

Sequencing Graphic Organizer

The sequencing graphic organizer below can be used before, during, and/or after reading a text. Have students focus on what is happening at the beginning, middle, and end of a passage. This organizer can assist below-grade-level students in recalling the texts. Depending on students' abilities, entries can be sketched, labeled, and/or written.

Beginning

```



```

Middle

```



```

End

```



```

Oral Storytelling

As an alternative to completing the graphic organizer above, students can orally retell what they learned from a text. This is a great comprehension strategy for below-grade-level students because it allows them to engage with texts while building listening and speaking skills. Oral storytelling is a great way for teachers to informally assess students' understanding of texts. Students can be prompted with the following questions: What happened first? Then what happened?

133

Strategies for Using the Leveled Texts *(cont.)*

Below-Grade-Level Students *(cont.)*

Frontloading Word Bags

Frontloading, or pre-teaching, vocabulary is a powerful tool for this student population. This strategy allows students who are below grade level to access content within a text through discussions beforehand. This can be a useful tool for students who struggle with on-demand activities. Select words from the text and place them in a bag prior to reading or introducing the text to students. Label the front of the bag with the title of the passage. Students can then work in a group or with the teacher to pull words out and discuss them. All questions and discussions should be focused on vocabulary comprehension and synthesizing words as they pertain to the main idea of each text.

Text	Words, Themes, and Content
Birds and Bugs	birds, bugs, owl, sit, branch, leaf, parrots, perch, lady, eat, leaves
My Birthday Party	birthday, friends, gifts, cupcakes, party
All About the Sun	sun, shine, melt, grow, warm, ice, help, bud, sprout, plants, flowers
Workers Who Take Care of Me	workers, take care, health, safety
Simple Tools	simple, tools, work, wheel, pull, heavy, easy, wagon, pulley, lift
The Bakery	bakery, sold, desserts, store, customer, left
In the Garden	garden, rabbits, snails, apples, ants, meadow, grass, leaf, ripe, lush
Farm Animals	big, small, cow, walk, meadow, chick, rabbit, flower, horse
Recess Time	slide, pattern, toy, park, school, short, tall, different, size, big, little
Fun in the Sun	tube, slide, ball, float, water, wear, goggles, pool, drop, twist, sand
On Land	grassy, sandy, wet, dry, hill, green, land, desert, very, swamp, crack
What Do Living Things Need?	light, food, water, air, sun, eat, drink
Baby Animals	bear, cub, duck, duckling, there, big, adult, little, playful, friend, fluffy
Solid or Liquid?	solid, liquid, this, orange, state, frozen, cream, melt
Changing Weather	sun, clouds, rain, rainbow, shine, gray, dark, wet, bright, colorful
I Am a Good Friend	help, share, play, together, care
Using Money	earn, count, save, spend, money, sell, lemonade
Map It!	map, place, looks, detail, find, type
Rules at Home	fair, share, nice, help, play, turn, family, chores
George Washington	George Washington, farmer, army, president, led, first

134

Strategies for Using the Leveled Texts *(cont.)*

Below-Grade-Level Students *(cont.)*

Graphic Organizer to Find Similarities and Differences

Setting a purpose for reading content focuses the learner. One purpose for reading can be to identify similarities and differences. This skill must be directly taught, modeled, and applied. Use the texts in this book to further students' understanding and/or to allow them to demonstrate what they know about a topic. For example, students could compare and contrast the *Rules at Home* passage to the rules in their own homes. Discussion questions can be questions such as the following: How are the rules in your home like the ones in the text? How are they different? The chart below can be used to respond to these questions.

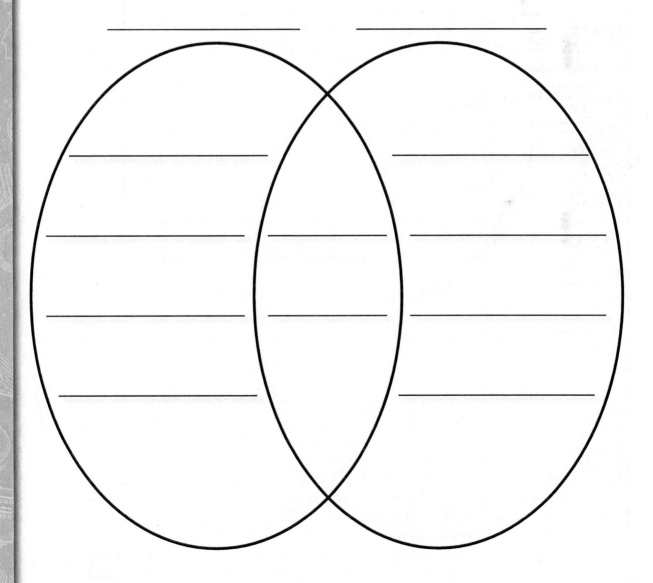

135

Strategies for Using the Leveled Texts (cont.)

Below-Grade-Level Students (cont.)

Sentence Frames

This is an underused technique that produces great results. Many below-grade-level students struggle with reading comprehension. They may need sentence frameworks to help them attack texts and gain confidence in discussing the material. Once students gain confidence and learn how to locate factual information, you phase out this technique.

There are two steps to successfully using this technique. First, use sentence prompts during discussions. Second, students use framed sentences when discussing and summarizing texts.

Examples of Sentence Frames

I think _____.   I notice _____.

The story is about _____.   I think _____ will happen next.

I learned _____.   In the beginning _____.

In the middle _____.   In the end _____.

Mapping the Main Idea

For nonfiction texts, students can use main idea maps. Combining the ideas behind Creative Mapping (Naughton 1993) and Semantic Mapping (Pearson and Johnson 1978), below-grade-level students can sketch or write about texts after previewing or reading. Have students complete the largest section on the map with the main idea. Prompt students to use titles and illustrations to do so. Next, students should add representations (visual or written) to represent the details that support the main idea. This strategy can be used before, during, or after reading a passage.

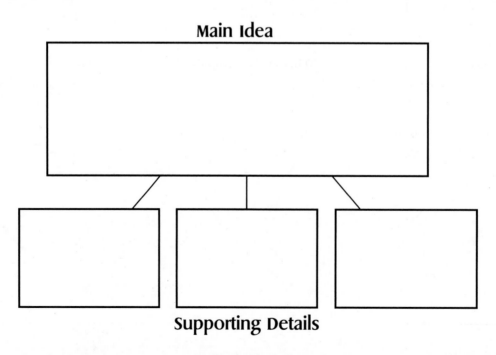

136

Strategies for Using the Leveled Texts *(cont.)*

On-Grade-Level Students

Questioning

Questioning is a great way for students to check their reading comprehension. This strategy can be student or teacher driven. After reading each text, have students pull one of the words from a bag and use the word to pose a question about the text to a classmate. Here are sample questions for the texts in this book:

| Who | takes care of animal babies? |

| What | patterns can you spot around us? |

| Where | do you live? |

| When | might you use a map? |

| Why | do we need tools? |

| How | can I earn and use money? |

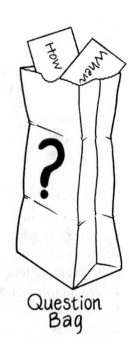

Question Bag

KWL

KWL charts empower students to take ownership of their learning. This strategy can be used as a pre- or post-reading tool for organizing what they've read or for further exploration for on-grade-level students. Guide students with the following questions:

- What does scanning the text tell us?
- What do you want to know about the topic?
- What do you know about the topic?
- What did you learn about the topic?

KWL Chart

What do I **know**? (K)	What do I **want** to learn? (W)	What did I **learn**? (L)

137

Strategies for Using the Leveled Texts *(cont.)*

Above-Grade-Level Students

Student-Directed Learning

Because they are academically advanced, above-grade-level students are often the leaders in primary classrooms. They are more self-sufficient learners, too. As a result, there are some student-directed strategies that teachers can employ successfully with these students. Remember to use the texts in this book as jump-starts so students will be interested in finding out more about the topics. Above-grade-level students may enjoy any of the following activities:

Reading and Writing Activities

- Write your own questions and exchange them with others.
- Craft your own story using the characters from the text.
- Read other texts about the topic to further expand your knowledge.
- Extend the plot of the story and write a new ending to the text.
- Research topics and write your own "All About" book.

Listening and Speaking Activity Activities

- Read the text and teach the topic to another group of students.
- Interview a friend about the topic read.

Art Activities

- Draw and label a detailed diagram of what you learned.
- Make a hand puppet to act out and retell the story.

Strategies for Using the Leveled Texts *(cont.)*

Above-Grade-Level Students *(cont.)*

Open-Ended Questions and Activities

Teachers need to be aware of activities that provide a ceiling that is too low for above-grade-level students. When given activities like this, these students become disengaged. These students can do more, but how much more? Offering open-ended questions and activities will provide above-grade-level students with opportunities to perform at or above their ability levels. For example, ask students to analyze the content described in the texts with questions such as: "In what ways do maps help people?" or "In what ways do simple tools help people?" These questions require students to form opinions, think deeply about the issues, and form statements in their minds. Questions like this have lots of right answers.

The generic open-ended question stems listed here can be adapted to any topic. These question stems can be used to develop comprehension questions for the leveled texts in this book.

- In what ways did . . .
- How might you have done this differently . . .
- What if . . .
- What are some possible explanations for . . .
- How does this affect . . .
- Explain several reasons why . . .
- What problems does this create . . .

- Describe the ways . . .
- What is the best . . .
- What is the worst . . .
- What is the likelihood . . .
- Predict the outcome . . .
- Support your reason . . .
- Make a plan for . . .
- Propose a solution . . .

Strategies for Using the Leveled Texts *(cont.)*

Above-Grade-Level Students *(cont.)*

Extension Activities

Extension activities can be used with above-grade-level students to build independence. All of these suggested extension ideas are geared towards research, presentation, crafts, and writing to extend the texts through classwork or as home/school connection assignments. (Note: All the passages do not have extension activities.)

Text	Extension Activity
My Birthday Party	Plan your next birthday celebration and make a list of the steps you need to take to get ready for the party.
All About the Sun	Conduct a science experiment to figure out what else the sun can do and how fast or slow it could melt or grow different things.
Workers Who Take Care of Me	Pick another worker who takes care of you and interview him/her. Create a list of your questions and their answers.
The Bakery	What if you had a bakery? Create a poster for all of the items you would sell. Don't forget to price each item.
In the Garden	Draw a garden with ten living things hidden in your picture. Test your friends to see if they can find all of the hidden pictures.
Recess Time	What are some patterns you see during recess? Draw a picture with five hidden patterns. See if your friends can find the patterns.
On Land	If you were an insect, which land would you like to live on? Pick one, sketch a picture, and write a story to go with your illustration.
What Do Living Things Need?	Create a poster using the information learned to explain what all living things need to survive. Make sure to label your diagram and present it to your class.
Solid or Liquid?	Draw 10 items on flash cards and ask your friends if each item is a solid or a liquid. See if they can get all 10 things correct.
I Am a Good Friend	Who is your best friend? Interview him or her and write a biography about his or her life. Make sure to include what makes him or her a good friend.
Using Money	What are some other ways you could earn money? What will you do with the money? Add another page to the text explaining your plan.
Map It!	Draw a map of your neighborhood. Be sure you label your house and all of your favorite places that you go with your family.

Strategies for Using the Leveled Texts (cont.)

English Language Learners

Vocabulary Work

Building academic vocabulary is essential for English language learners. This strategy can be used before or after reading a text. Start your discussion for each text by asking students about each word that they will encounter in the text. Teachers can print the words and have a visual image of each word. Allowing English language leaners to encounter text prior to the on-demand activity will aid in fluency, build confidence, and allow students opportunities to process content and focus on comprehension rather than decoding while reading. A list of suggested vocabulary words from the texts in this book is included on page 134.

Picture Dictionary

As an extension to the vocabulary activity, students can make picture dictionaries. Illustrating text-specific words can help students make visual connections to words in the texts. As students are reading the texts, they can look at picture clues to assist with text meaning.

_____'s **Picture Dictionary**	_____	_____

Strategies for Using the Leveled Texts (cont.)

English Language Learners (cont.)

Practice Concepts and Language Objectives

English language learners need to practice what they learn through engaging activities. Some people retain knowledge better after applying what they learn to their own lives. This is definitely true for many English language learners. Students can apply content and language knowledge by creating projects, stories, skits, poems, or artifacts that show what they learned. Some activities should be geared to the right side of the brain, like those listed above. For students who are left-brain dominant, activities such as defining words and concepts, using graphic organizers, and explaining procedures should be developed.

Interview

Students may interview members of their families or neighbors to obtain information regarding a topic from the texts in this book. For example: What types of plants do you eat?

Home/School Connection

The home/school connection is an important component in the learning process for English language learners. Parents are students' first teachers, and they establish expectations for their children. These expectations help shape the behavior of their children. By asking parents to be active participants in the education of their children, students get double doses of support and encouragement. As a result, families become partners, and chances for success in your classroom increase. You can send home copies of the texts in this book for parents to read with their children. You can even send multiple levels to meet the needs of your second-language parents as well as your students. In this way, you are sharing what you are covering in class with your whole second-language community.

Strategies for Using the Leveled Texts *(cont.)*

English Language Learners *(cont.)*

Cause and Effect

This cause-and-effect graphic organizer will assist English language learners to "see" the relationships between causes and effects in the texts read. The texts and prompts below can be used to utilize this graphic organizer.

Text Title	Cause
My Birthday Party	The twins have a birthday coming up . . .
All About the Sun	The sun is hot . . .
Simple Tools	You need to lift something heavy . . .
Solid or Liquid?	Ice gets warm . . .

Cause	Effect

Resources

Contents of the Digital Resource CD

PDF Files

The full-color PDFs provided are each six pages long and contain all three levels of a reading passage. For example, *Birds and Bugs* PDF (pages 11–16) is the *birds.pdf* file.

Text Files

The Microsoft Word® documents include the text for all three levels of each reading passage. For example, *Birds and Bugs* text (pages 11–16) is the *birds.docx* file.

Text Title	Text File	PDF
Birds and Bugs	birds.docx	birds.pdf
My Birthday Party	birthday.docx	birthday.pdf
All About the Sun	sun.docx	sun.pdf
Workers Who Take Care of Me	workers.docx	workers.pdf
Simple Tools	tools.docx	tools.pdf
The Bakery	bakery.docx	bakery.pdf
In the Garden	garden.docx	garden.pdf
Farm Animals	animals.docx	animals.pdf
Recess Time	recess.docx	recess.pdf
Fun in the Sun	funsun.docx	funsun.pdf
On Land	land.docx	land.pdf
What Do Living Things Need?	livingthings.docx	livingthings.pdf
Baby Animals	baby.docx	baby.pdf
Solid or Liquid?	solidor.docx	solidor.pdf
Changing Weather	weather.docx	weather.pdf
I Am a Good Friend	friend.docx	friend.pdf
Using Money	money.docx	money.pdf
Map It!	map.docx	map.pdf
Rules at Home	rulesathome.docx	rulesathome.pdf
George Washington	washington.docx	washington.pdf

Word Documents of Texts

- Change leveling further for individual students.
- Separate text and images for students who need additional help decoding the text.
- Resize the text for visually impaired students.

Digital Resource CD

Full-Color PDFs of Texts

- Project texts for whole-class review.
- Post on your website and read texts online.
- Email texts to parents or students at home.

144